FREEDOM
WITHOUT
PERMISSION

HOW TO LIVE FREE IN A WORLD THAT ISN'T

Table of Contents

Preface and Acknowledgement

This collection is the result of a series of conversations between friends about the practical implications of liberty. Each of us approaches what it means to exist as a free being from our own perspectives, understanding that each individual comes into this world with a presumption of liberty over their own life. Unless you choose to cede control of your life to somebody else, you are the one in the driver's seat.

Unfortunately, many decide to hand over control to somebody else. They do this both consciously and unconsciously. Through a mindset of pessimistic determinism, putting too much weight in politics, waiting until schools or colleagues tell them they are allowed to go after their dreams, or by simply waiting around and living life unconsciously, individuals give up the greatest experience over which they exert direct control: their lives.

We engage with some of these areas in the pages within.

Thanks to James Walpole for assistance in copyediting the final proof.

Introduction

This book is not about how to "fake it until you make it" with freedom. It is not about how to pretend to feel free or how to learn to be happy and accept a boot on your neck. It's about your worldview — the lens through which you view and interpret the world. We are not looking to leave you with a unique theory of political philosophy.

We are looking to help you find freedom on the individual level. You either see yourself as the fundamental locus of control over your life or you see some external force as in control. We suggest that the former is true, but you have to understand and accept it as true before you can reap the benefits.

Many people live in unconscious denial of this truth and instead behave as if they are not free unless given permission by others. This is only true to the extent to which they live it. They relinquish the reality of their own power over their life by believing they don't have it. Giving mental assent to people or systems that pretend to control you allows them to do just that.

We do not pretend that there is no world outside of your mind. The real world does in fact exist. Hurricanes are real. Cancer is real. Violence and coercion are real. The question is not whether these exist or have the ability to impact you. They certainly do. The question is this: *how you will respond or, better yet, how you will preemptively think and act to reduce unwanted effects of these things?* From what orientation will you see and experience the world? How will you navigate around these realities to create your journey? It begins with acknowledging that though you can't control the seas, you are steering the ship.

We wish to challenge the mindset that follows dominant paths, believes common narratives, and waits to be told what's allowed, often without even realizing it. We wish to help in the process of your mental emancipation. This is not a blueprint or guide to constructing a free life but rather a wrecking ball to smash barriers to doing so. We intend to help you discover mental models and assumptions that are stifling your freedom and fulfillment. Once discovered and demolished, only you can step into the light and build the kind of life you want to live.

The key to doing this is being motivated by your own desire to be free. Freedom works first and best when it is personal and individual.

The subject matter covered in this collection may at first appear disparate, but there is a common theme and a logical progression. The chapters become progressively abstract and personal. The first two chapters deal with historical freedom and gaining freedom *from* politics and affecting social change in the political realm. The next chapter, "Freedom in Education and Career," pertains to the social institutions which influence our educational and career choices. It deals with the way these institutions influence you and how you can navigate them, or avoid them entirely. The last chapter, "Keeping It Real," explores the constraints that we place on ourselves and our own ability to create a narrative that we are happy to live.

We tackle common areas in which people start from a permission-based mindset, from disempowering beliefs about the need for political reform, to intellectual life, to work and personal development, and many things in between. Being free without permission is a process. It's not something you achieve once for all. If you're reading this, you're already working on it. Keep it up, with or without anyone's permission.

Freedom Without Permission as Self-Governance
Christopher Nelson

Who is against freedom? Everyone likes it. Everyone wants it. But how do we get it? What does it mean to have it? How does one actually live freely? Is it just about political freedom? What about freedom beyond politics, like in our day-to-day life?

Knowing that you're already free is an important first step. Actually living freely is the next.

Captain Levi Preston, who fought at Lexington, was interviewed many decades after the American Revolution. His answers to the question of why it was worth the fighting for are remarkable:

> When the action at Lexington, on the morning of the 19th [of April], was known at Danvers, the minute men there, under the lead of Captain Gideon Foster, made that memorable march--or run, rather--of sixteen miles in four

hours, and struck Percy's flying column at West Cambridge. Brave but incautious in flanking the Redcoats, they were flanked themselves and badly pinched, leaving seven dead, two wounded, and one missing. Among those who escaped was Levi Preston, afterwards known as Captain Levi Preston.

When I was about twenty-one and Captain Preston about ninety-one, I interviewed him as to what he did and thought sixty-seven years before, on April 19, 1775. And now, fifty-two years later, I make my report--a little belated perhaps, but not too late, I trust, for the morning papers!

With an assurance passing even that of the modern interviewer--if that were possible--I began:

'Captain Preston, why did you go to the Concord fight, the 19th of April, 1775?'

The old man, bowed beneath the weight of years, raised himself upright, and turning to me said:

'Why did I go?'

'Yes,' I replied; 'my histories tell me that you men of the Revolution took up arms against 'intolerable oppressions.' What were they?
Oppressions?'

'I didn't feel them.'

'What, were you not oppressed by the Stamp Act?'

'I never saw one of those stamps, and always understood that Governor Bernard [of Massachusetts] put them all in Castle William [Boston]. I am certain I never paid a penny for one of them.'

'Well, what then about the tea-tax?'

'Tea-tax! I never drank a drop of the stuff; the boys threw it all overboard.'

'Then I suppose you had been reading Harrington or Sidney and Locke about the eternal principles of liberty.'

'Never heard of 'em. We read only the Bible, the Catechism, Watts' Psalms and Hymns, and the Almanack.'

'Well, then, what was the matter? and what did you mean in going to the fight?'

'Young man, what we meant in going for those Redcoats was this: *we always had governed ourselves, and we always meant to. They didn't mean we should.*'[1]

Captain Preston knew he was free. That intellectual leap was crucial. But being free wasn't simply about throwing off the British Empire. He was free because for generations he and his fellow North Americans had been freely governing themselves already. They hadn't waited for anyone's permission to get that freedom or to receive confirmation that they were free.

Despite what we hear in our history classes, the Revolution didn't create America. The Declaration and subsequent struggle was simply a reminder to the British of the ways in which the civilization that already grown on the continent

---

[1] Sisson, Edward. *America The Great*. Amazon Digital Services. Amazon Kindle. Quotation marks and emphasis added.

had always governed itself — and always intended to.

Self-governance as a framework for living a permission-free life

We can debate all day about politics. What are we ultimately aiming at in these debates?

Self-governance.

There are those who intend to rule and those who fight against being ruled.

I want to explore self-governance as a way in which to be free. I'll talk about what self-governance is, the steps to getting and keeping it, and responses to challenges and confusion over what it's all about.

As noted, no one is *really* against freedom. Everyone thinks that what they're hoping to achieve, whether politically or personally, is some greater degree of freedom. Who wants to be constrained? Though many policies might unintentionally lead to more restrictions on freedom, few actively seek to put themselves under greater constraints. But even self-described freedom fighters sometimes unintentionally place themselves under constraints. Part of the reason for this is not knowing what they're ultimately aiming at.

There's no Utopia. There's no point at which freedom has been perfectly achieved. It's not a destination. It's a constant struggle. That's why it's worth the strategic challenge of thinking through the value of not having to ask for it in the first place. But having a goal in mind matters greatly to measuring how you're doing trying to get somewhere near freedom.

Disagreements about strategies and tactics often lack a relative objective to comparatively measure one approach over another. If you want more ice cream, you can debate about how nice you ought to be to the ice cream man or what approaches to take in general to getting ice cream. But imagine if you never decided on what ice cream place you wanted to visit or that you even wanted ice cream at all. If the vague idea entered people's minds that dessert mattered, with ice cream being the secret desire, people might fight over tactics and just settle with brownies.

Similarly, unless you have a sense of what that freedom looks like or at what point you've achieved it, the success and failure of tactics and strategies are going to be difficult to measure.

Debates about anarchists versus limited government are notoriously challenging. They often erupt into mud-slinging over who is best serving the cause of freedom because of disagreements over tactics and strategies. But what these debates often lack is a sense of where either side is hoping to go.

The anarchists are explicitly clear: the less state the better — no state is best. Limited government people want less government, but *less than what?* The US has less government than China. China has less government than North Korea. Is China a limited government? Arguing about how to convince the Chinese government to decrease its size will necessitate certain strategies and tactics only to the extent to which you're clear about how far you want to go.

But why does this matter for not asking for freedom?

Perhaps we all need a better target.

Though much of the debate about tactics is implicitly about whether we can even define a goal, let's try one on for size: self-governance.

Self-governance is both the space within which you're practicing freedom and the reason you're already in a position to not need another's permission.

You're already doing it.

If the government of China is huge, but its distance to you has meant you're already making decisions on your own, you're halfway there. If you already believe that what you're doing is both desirable and possible, you've made it all the way.

Aspects of self-governance: believing you're free and living a free life

Captain Preston knew he was free. He also lived like he was free. He and his generation practiced that belief by knowing they'd gotten to where they were by practicing self-governance, and they continued to live like self-governance mattered.

It's not clear which needs to come first. Was Preston free because he had the space to practice governing himself? Was he able to assert his personal freedom because he'd proved to himself and the British that he didn't need to be governed by anyone else?

Or did he assert his freedom first, then have to learn to be actually free and govern himself? While these three steps — asserting freedom, realizing you don't need to ask permission, and then actually living freely — are necessary, it's not necessarily clear that they have to happen in some particular order. Though it's sometimes believed that only people worthy of freedom can be free, Adam Smith showed us in his 1776 *An Inquiry Into the Nature and Causes of the Wealth of Nations* that it's not by the benevolence of others that people get fed. The amazing thing about a world of self-governing institutions like markets is that they require very little to work beyond people pursuing their own self-governing activities.

That's not to say self-governance is easy. It takes practice. But having the space to practice it and admitting that you're free by virtue of your existence to have that space to practice it are what matter. We don't have to insist we're something we're not to appease those from whom we feel compelled to seek permission.

There are numerous points in life when, whether we want to or not, we actually need to govern ourselves. Despite the disposition of those who intend to rule as governors over others, classical liberal sociologists from Alexis de Tocqueville, author of *Democracy in America*, to German thinkers like Franz Oppenheimer, author of *The State*, and Alexander Rüstow, author of *Freedom and Domination*, have observed the distance between the rulers and ruled. Those presumed to be ruled, whether they've made intellectual leaps like Preston about their inherent freedom or not, quite simply need to take care of themselves. Governments can claim to be the only ones delivering the goods, but it would be impossible to count the myriad ways in which they fail to live up to their self-imposed charge.

The British Empire sought no permission and simply claimed its benevolent authority to protect North America before the Revolution. But it was the generations of North Americans that came before Preston that did the heavy lifting, not the faraway Parliament or Crown across the Atlantic.

Homeschoolers, concerned for their children's education, haven't waited for schools to meet their standards. They've had to educate their children the best way they know how.

People in love haven't waited for states to recognize their matrimony. They've fallen for each other and lived as couples anyway.

As it happens, the rulers whose permission many believe we ought to seek create numerous gaps in their authority that require and implicitly allow us to live freely regardless of their desires.

Living freely, whether because you've asserted your freedom or because you've had to govern yourself out of necessity, has beneficial effects for others hoping to live a life without permission. Buried within the arguments those who claim to hold authority make about how the rest of us must wait for permission is a view about whether those who are ruled even can live freely.

Many in the British Empire believed that without the British in North America, the continent would turn into a mess.

Many believe that with individuals acting on their own in the marketplace, unchecked, the economy would be ruined.

Many think that the only education one can receive is the one given to them by those with authorized credentials.

And even those with the capacity to live freely, that is, practice self-governance, might believe that they are philosophically free to live such a life, but that in the "real world," it might be admittedly hard to do it. Still others who think they are by right and ought to be free and who are convinced that self-governance is possible might simply think that proving to others, including the rulers, that the rest of us can live freely will be impossible. This is usually where disagreements about whether we need permission break down into how best to argue, persuade, and convince others, rather than simply continuing to live freely.

Self-governance is both a way of living and its very own best advertisement for how great self-governance is. Captain Preston's generation lived and always intended to live freely. They did that without the British and despite their claims. For anyone in their day who wondered whether the British were necessary to North America's survival, they only needed to read the interview with Preston above — or just look around.

We don't need someone's permission for something we're already doing. We don't need the help of someone else when we're able to accomplish something on our own. We just need to take a chance on ourselves and admit that living freely is not only desirable but possible.

Political Freedom: Achieving Freedom from Politics

Zachary Slayback

Political freedom is the most obvious and pressing type of freedom, and for good reason. Lack of political freedom resulted in the deaths of more than 170,000,000 people in the first 88 years of the 20th Century alone.[2] To this day, unfree political institutions across the globe harass, beat, kidnap, maim, extort, torture, bomb, shoot, and kill people living within and outside their borders.

Political unfreedom is a very real thing.

Yet this is not the kind of unfreedom I am interested in here.

Political institutions exert another sort of unfreedom on those concerned with their governance: *psychological unfreedom.*

This sort is particularly prevalent in western liberal societies like the United States, where

---

[2] Rummel, R.J.. *Death by Government*. New Brunswick, NJ. Transaction Publishers. 1997. Print.

electoral politics plays a huge role in the media and in day-to-day conversations about freedom. The irony about these conversations is that this unfreedom comes about precisely when one constantly searches for freedom in the political process.

When you put all hope in broadening the sphere of personal freedom in the political process — particularly in electoral politics — you move the responsibility for freedom from your own hands and into the hands of politicians, bureaucrats, lobbyists, and campaign managers.

Libertarians are particularly prone to falling into this trap. They are not alone, though. Conservatives and progressives who exert real labor on the political process and who are emotionally distraught over the opinions of this or that politician or by a policy decision that will probably never impact them also fall into this trap.

The most obvious ways in which this worldview is enslaving is when people get emotionally upset at friends and family who hold different political views than they do, or at policy minutia that will barely affect them, or at the comments of some politician on the other side of the country.

Where somebody devotes emotional energy and how that is expressed can provide a window into how they prioritize their expectations and desires of the world.

The goal of this section is to elucidate why this emphasis on the traditional political process is doomed to practical failure, emotional frustration, and broken relationships. It is also to provide ways of breaking free from this mindset and focusing on different avenues to achieve the sense of freedom in one's life that is lost in the political process.

We look at the problems with effecting change through the electoral process, the ways in which politics negatively affects our relationships with others, and finally the root causes of emotional frustrations with politics.

Your vote doesn't matter

Fast forward to election season. Somebody marches out a sign or an advertisement telling voters, "Your vote matters!" and "You can make a difference!" The message behind these is clear: every vote matters and what you believe can be reflected in politics by casting your ballot today.

The only problem with this is that this isn't true.

You are more likely to be killed on your ways to the polls than to affect the outcome of a major national election. The likelihood of actually being that vote that matters — the one vote on the margin — is very low.

This can be illustrated on a much smaller level. Imagine going to a group restaurant with 400 friends and voting between two or three options to order for dinner for everybody. The likelihood of the voting coming down to 200 vs. 200 is so small and we would think it just wouldn't happen. Now imagine going to the same restaurant with 80,000,000 friends and choosing between two options. Now the likelihood is mind-bogglingly small.

The first step to removing the anxiety and unfreedom of politics from your life is to recognize that who you vote for literally cannot determine the outcome of the election.

Don't stress over which candidate to vote for. It doesn't matter.

Rational ignorance is bliss

National policy is a really complex thing. State policy is complex. Even school district policy can be complicated. It's no wonder, then, that most voters are totally uninformed about the intricacies of issues their political institutions are attempting to handle and that candidates run on.

Voters are ignorant. And that's okay.

Most voters realize there are better things to spend most of their time on than politics. These are things that make people happier or have a bigger impact on their lives. If you're like most people, spending time with your family will make you happier than reading up on energy policy. Spending your time figuring out how the back-wiper on your car works will make a bigger impact in your personal life than knowing your senatorial candidate's position on the farm subsidies bill.

This is what economists call *rational igno-rance.*

Despite what your 9th grade civics teacher told you, being ignorant of politics doesn't make you a bad person. Time is scarce and people need to ration it and spend it on the things from which they get the most satisfaction. Most people see politics as something detached from themselves — even in the voting booth — and see many things closer to them that are more pressing. To choose the pressing, closer things within one's own sphere of influence over non-urgent things outside of one's sphere is com-pletely rational.

Imagine how much more stressful life would be if our political positions were actually called into action and questioned just as often as the decisions we make for our families, loved ones, or even our diets. Even the political savant would have an intense increase in day-to-day anxiety.

The quality of your life and mine are much greater because we can pick and choose the things we pay attention to. The political savant gets joy out of knowing the ins and outs of poli-tics just as the sports fan may, but such an in-depth knowledge doesn't affect the outcomes in either case.

We shouldn't want voting to matter

Most voters actually hold positions which prevent them from *voting well*. If voting does matter, then it would follow that we ought to vote well. Cognitive biases prevent most people from voting well, meaning that the policies they tend to select for end up making society worse-off, either economically, socially, or morally.

Bryan Caplan, an economist at George Mason University, identifies at least four of these biases in his work on voting.[3]

These biases include:

Anti-foreign bias — The idea of ending trade restrictions to open up free trade sounds great to most people until they are told that this means that some jobs, like manufacturing positions, will be moved to foreign lands . Any election cycle is rife with hit ads that say that one (if not both) of the candidates "wants to move

3 Caplan, Bryan. *The Myth of the Rational Voter*, Princeton, NJ. Princeton University Press. 2007. Print.

American jobs overseas." What this bias misses is that the gains from trade are always greater than the gains from restrictions. (This applies to a market in labor, too — most people are opposed to loosening immigration restrictions under the same bias.)

Make-work bias — Whenever anybody talks about cutting back a government program or moving government services to the private sector, whether they be teaching positions, mail-delivery, emergency services, or military protection, people assume this means getting rid of these things. They only look for the immediate consequences of policy, rather than the lateral unseen consequences.

Anti-market bias — "Deregulation," especially since the Great Recession, is a dirty word to many voters' ears. They imagine Monopoly Men running about, subjugating hard workers, putting mom-and-pop shops out of business, and making life generally worse-off. The reality is that this bias is manifested with price controls (e.g., rent control, calls for surge-pricing controls on ride-sharing services, price ceilings on milk and bread, etc.). The benefactors of these policies are entrenched interests. Large, corporate rent-seeking farms are the benefactors of agriculture subsidies, not your home-town farmer.

Pessimistic bias — Any glance at the daily news illustrates this bias. Voters like to focus on how things are getting worse. The economy is getting worse. Schools are getting worse. The world is becoming a more dangerous place for children/minorities/women/any identity group.

These biases create incentives for politicians to pursue policies that reflect them. Plenty of politicians are happy to argue for tariffs or for policies to "keep American jobs American," even though almost every economist from Paul Krugman to Thomas Sowell agrees that globalization makes everybody better off.

Let's illustrate what I mean by "voting well."

Imagine participating in a 100-person firing squad that is to execute an innocent 7 year old girl. You know that your pulling the trigger won't make the difference in whether or not the girl is executed. Would you still participate? Or would you choose not to participate in something that results in such a terrible thing?[4]

Even if your vote doesn't matter, participating in a process that creates perverse incentives for policies that make very real people substantively worse off is reason to release yourself from the anxiety of electoral politics. If voting did matter, we wouldn't want most people to vote anyway, since the incentives at play create a high likelihood of people selecting for destructive policies.

Public choice: the public rarely chooses

"My vote doesn't matter, sure. But voting as a whole matters! We give politicians a mandate of the people in elections!"

Perhaps. Voting as a whole does have an impact on the way politics goes, but not necessarily because of the way in which people vote.

Voting matters only insofar as it is the means by which politicians retain or lose their jobs.

---

[4] I take this thought experiment from Brennan, Jason. *The Ethics of Voting.* Princeton, NJ. Princeton University Press. 2012. Print.

This is important because it is key to shifting the way we conceive of electoral politics from a 9th-grade-civics framework to a reality-based framework. Politicians are like everybody else — self-interested.

The idea that there is a "mandate of the people," or that politicians are elected to serve some cause outside of themselves is simply not reflected in reality. Politicians are self-interested first and foremost and serve other apparent interests only when those interests happen to coincide with their own.

This goes against the traditional story of politician-as-public-servant and finds its roots in economic analysis.

The Virginia School of economics — known as such for its roots at Virginia-based institutions — applies the *homo economicus* model to political actors. *Homo economicus*, or "economic man," is a model for thinking about actors in the marketplace that conceives of them as primarily self-interested utility maximizers. This is the traditional model used for economic analyses of marketplace exchanges. This doesn't mean that politicians are by-nature evil — it simply means they are like you and I. They want to keep their jobs and get the most out of them if possible. If that aligns with the public interest, that's great.

Politicians must work a balancing act between supporting policies that their voters won't boot them out over and policies supported by special interests. It is as if they are at a table at a restaurant and have a menu in front of them and two people with them, both of whom they must satisfy, with 30 options to choose. One of the people says he approves of options 1-20, while they other says she approves of options 18-30. The politician will then choose options 18, 19, or 20.

To use an example from above, agriculture subsidies are unlikely to go away anytime soon for this reason. Voters like the idea of subsidies to farmers, and the agriculture lobby is more than happy to target politicians up for reelection who oppose their policies.

This isn't some nefarious conspiracy — it's just economics. If a group X can gain $1,000,000 from the passage of a new subsidy or regulation, then it is rational for them to spend up to $999,999.99 in getting it passed.

On the other side of the coin, the same policy may only cost each person in the country less than a third of a cent per year. If it costs them so little, then it isn't surprising when they don't feel passionately about the policy.

You can illustrate all the economic inefficiencies and deadweight loss caused by a policy, you can remonstrate with friends and relatives about how immoral the policy is, you can even show them real examples of the harm the policy causes, but it will prove to be very difficult to overwhelm the efforts of special interests who gain concentrated benefits from dispersing costs over many people.

Change comes in politics when an electorate starts changing what they want on the "menu." Through experience, voters change the ideas they have that determine their implicit beliefs.When this happens, voters may very well start saying "no" or "yes" to more options.

For a long time, supporting the legalization of same-sex marriage was not a politically tenable position for most politicians outside of California and New England. On the "menu" of options, legal same-sex marriage was option 3, and voters only approved of options 4-6. To further complicate things, a traditional values lobby would only support options 5-8, so politicians were opposed to liberalization efforts on the whole.

As culture shifted over time and more people saw that the hysteria around same-sex marriage was probably misguided, as they saw that their gay neighbors were not some kind of social deviants, and as they saw leaders in culture embrace liberalization, they eventually made it politically feasible for politicians to choose option 3. Over time, this support also gave birth to an LGBT lobby to counter the efforts of a waning traditional lobby.

The individual vote in this matter didn't change the way politicians voted. Even those voters who supported more liberal efforts would have been counteracted by special interests supporting more conservative efforts. It was through experience, not voting, that the menu of options shifted.

The perpetual government

Electoral outcomes determine which politicians hold elected office. These politicians then have lacks who draft the legislation, and the politicians take it debate and vote. This legislation may have very real consequences outside of the political world. A farm subsidy bill may determine whether or not a town gets hundreds of thousands of tax dollars, a surveillance bill may set the legal standards for a whole industry, and a declaration of war really does make the difference between life and death for many.

This government changes over time, though. Parties and agendas shift between elections, different issues get different airtime, and there may very well be progress or recession between categories.

There's a separate government that doesn't change nearly as easily: the bureaucracy.

While voters as a group may be able to exert some kind of control over the makeup of the legislature, the executive, and (indirectly) the judiciary, the bureaucracy remains constant and unaccountable to any particular electoral outcome. Different electoral outcomes may play a role in which bureaucrats are appointed as positions become vacant, but a widespread dissatisfaction with the policies of the IRS is not going to result in IRS agents and employees losing their jobs or changing their policies to satiate public concerns.

Legislation really just determines the direction or ends to which government programs aim. It is the bureaucracy which determines the means to those ends. It is rarely the politician who harasses the business owner, the scientist, or the artist, but rather the bureaucrat. The bureaucrat, whose job it is to make countable that which was not formerly and to maintain records for government programs, issues books upon books of regulations, not the politician.

Rescinding the roles of the bureaucrats requires even more political force than simply rescinding a bad government program. Not only must a politician be incentivized by voters to roll back the program the bureaucrats are in charge of, but he must also be incentivized to such a level as to outweigh the special interests of the bureaucrats themselves. Like any other group of people, bureaucrats will lobby, either directly or indirectly, to support their jobs. They will oppose the positions looking to roll back the programs they support and use anti-market bias and make-work bias to convince voters and politicians that rolling back the program would do more harm than good. Sizing down the perpetual government and undoing bureaucratic overreach is a project in itself.

The fruitlessness of electoral politics becomes blatant when one looks behind the curtain and sees the bureaucrat, not the politician.

Think of schools. Sizing down a school is one of the hardest political moves one can make. Not only do people conflate schools with education, but they also happen to know a lot of people who are employed by schools. Those people have friends, family, and a union behind them to fight against downsizing. They'll put out the full-force of their agenda to keep the school from getting downsized — it's their livelihoods on the line, after all.

Politics makes us worse friends

Despite the fact that most people aren't very well-informed on policy matters, they do hold initial beliefs — intuitions — that lead to political opinions. These political opinions can be quite strong.

Thanks to a civic culture that directly connects what you vote for to your personal values, these opinions are further emphasized as matters of self-identity. We get "red states" and "blue states," "conservatives," "progressives," and "independents," and people start to think of themselves in such terms.

Add to this mix a never-ending election season and a media that feeds off streaming political news constantly, rather than our interests, hobbies, passions, and goals.

We begin to see our friends and colleagues who have differing political opinions than us as somehow worse people. "Surely they believe in that policy because they have corrupt values!" "How can he not see that Senator Johnson is a shill for big oil!" "Why can't she understand that economic development is more humane than environmental conservation?"

Politics turns friends into enemies by taking intuitions — oftentimes not very well-vetted ones — and bringing them to the fore of a person's role in society.

By releasing our own personal reliance on the political system as a means to achieving our ideal life, we can help maintain our relationships. This is in fact the very first step to repairing relationships damaged due to politics.

When you start viewing other systems — educational, entrepreneurial, or social — as the primary vehicles of achieving your goals and your ideal life, the influence you place on another person's political values and how this may reflect on them as people naturally wanes. Seeing your friend as an artist rather than as a progressive or a conservative fosters less contempt, resentment, and frustration.

Emotional freedom from politics

The contempt, resentment, and frustration felt towards political news, outcomes, and relationships is a natural consequence of holding strong expectations on the political process.

In the field of moral psychology, a subset of emotions called the reactive attitudes are defined by our expectations of the world and violations of those expectations. Usually, these attitudes are used as mechanisms for us to stand up for ourselves and to enforce moral norms.

When you are on the subway, you have a reasonable expectation that you won't have your foot needlessly stepped on by other riders. When another rider steps on your foot, you resent him. He has violated an expectation that you and others within the subway understand.

The same goes for our relationships. Informal relationships like friendships and acquaintanceships are regulated by norms and expectations for what friends do for each other. If you've ever found yourself saying, "well, that's just what friends do for each other!" (either in exasperation or joy), you understand this to be true. Your friend who flakes on dinner garners your resentment for violating the expectation that friends will actually show up at agreed-upon times.

In a formal relationship like a business partnership or a marriage, the expectations are clear and explicit. Violations of these oftentimes lead to emotional damage and the relationship being hurt.

This holds true for our relation to the political realm. When we expect a politician to carry through on a campaign promise and they don't, we resent them. When they violate an informal expectation we had — one that wasn't made explicit by a promise but one that we anticipate them to follow anyway — we resent them. We find ourselves being more and more frustrated as our expectations of the political process a means of social change are not met.

On the flip-side, this also explains why people feel a sense of gratitude when a political actor does something that lives up to an expectation or goes above and beyond it.

Think of the amount of respect just being honest garners most politicians in America today. We've come to have a negative expectation of the honesty of politicians, so when they actually violate this negative expectation and do something positive, many actually feel gracious, even though being honest is itself the formal expectation.

Again, this extends to why we feel so resentful towards friends, colleagues, and family who hold differing political positions. We expect them, being good and moral people with whom we associate, to reflect that in their political beliefs. When they don't, we not only feel surprised but actually a little bit resentful.

Doing away with this resentment starts first with releasing the expectations at the core of it. If we no longer expect politics to be an effective means of bringing about the world we want to live in, then we can't and won't feel surprised when politicians fail us. If we release this expectation, the expectation that others must hold our own beliefs to be good is released as a follow-up. Who cares if your mother is a raging progressive when you yourself don't expect anything from politics?

Political atheism

In this sense, the person who does not get frustrated over politics — the person who has released their expectations from politicians and the political process — is akin to an atheist. An atheist doesn't resent a deity or force in the universe when bad fortune comes his way because he doesn't expect any such deity or force to exert control over the universe.

If we want to make our lives more emotionally and psychologically free and fulfilled, we ought to become political atheists. When we see problems in the world around us, rather than defaulting to, "there ought to be a law," we look elsewhere. We create solutions, not vote for them. We need not take up a quasi-religious rite of praising politicians at the voting altar to bring about the world we want to live in — expecting to do as much usually leads to resentment and frustration.

Freeing yourself from politics starts with letting go of the expectation that politicians are public servants who are sure to follow the edict of the individual voter. Once this expectation is gone, all others oriented around the political follow.

Freedom in Education and Career
Isaac Morehouse

Living free without permission requires the adoption of new paradigms and, more importantly, the destruction of old. I'll outline several myths and modes of thought that engender the permission-based approach to life, from education through career, and suggest ways to free yourself from them.

Let's break some stuff.

Education vs. school

The major paradigm you must first shatter is the conflation of education[5] with school.

---

[5] The word "Education" feels a bit narrow, boring, and baggage-laden to me. It often conveys the type of rigidness I'm setting out to shatter. It'd be more accurate, though less quick and catchy, to call it something like learning, growing, producing and exchanging. These are all ongoing processes. They're fun, challenging, dynamic, and utterly unique based on each person's preferences and goals. Despite its connotations, I'll use the word education. If you don't like it, don't let it distract. Feel free to substitute your own.

It seems funny to say you don't need permission to become educated. In fact, most young people don't think anyone is holding them back from learning. Quite the opposite. They're forced to "get an education," and what they really need permission for is not to learn, but to play, have fun, and be left alone. This reveals just how backward our mindset is with regard to education. A Google image search for the word results in desks, chalkboards, letter grades, stressed students, regimentation, classrooms, and kids sleeping or with pained looks on their faces. But that's not education at all. That's school.

Education is the process of learning. Learning happens everywhere. It can happen in schools, but the structure and incentives in the school system reward only a very narrow type of learning which is often the kind least valuable to your freedom and happiness. School is about becoming compliant and obedient, performing tasks without questioning the value, and jumping through hoops you didn't create to reach made up ends you never sought. School is about pain avoidance, not passion-seeking. It's the opposite of freedom in every way. Prisoners and school children keep essentially the same schedules, except the kids go home after classes and other structured activities and swap out wardens – parents replace teachers in demanding forced learning, often taking the side of the schools by default in this antagonistic relationship. This is not a recipe for the kind of education you actually want for your own life and goals.

Schooling and the worldview that goes with it is actually about reducing education. Most schools were established to do just that. Though highly literate, children were not uniform enough for social engineers and do-gooders. There were, frankly, too many ideas and too many forms of education. The supply was too great, not too little. School was designed to replace the myriad market options in education with a single monolith that spat out a social widget to be plugged in wherever planners saw best for "society" or "country." It was never about the individual student getting where they wanted to go in life but about being a cog in some control-freak's imagined utopia. Screw that.

"Because I have to"

There are a growing number of people who see the huge difference between education and school. Parents are disgusted by the soul-crushing regimentation of schools and students find the debt-fueled four-year party called college annoying and wasteful. The saddest part is that so many of those who get it still don't really get it.

The number one response I get when I ask young people why they're going to college is "because I have to." Consider remarks like these:

"College is such a huge waste for me. My professors are terrible, fellow students just party all the time, I'm going into debt and gaining no skills of interest or value to me I couldn't get better, faster, and cheaper on my own. Oh well, time to sign up for the next semester. I wish every job didn't require a degree, but it does."

"My kid hates school. The teachers keep trying to put her on Ritalin. Classmates make fun of her. She's not learning and she's become more withdrawn. She sometimes cries after school. It really makes me sad to know I've got to drop her off there again tomorrow. I hope it starts to get better with this new teacher."

In cases like these, the problem has been diagnosed, but there is resignation to an unhappy fate, as if these students and parents are waiting for some external savior to swoop in and change the way things are "in society."

Guess what? You don't need to wait for society to get there. You can opt out immediately and create a better way for yourself. (As a secondary benefit, doing so is the most likely way for a broader social movement to follow).

What to do? It's a lot easier than you think.

Quit.

Opt out of the activities and mindsets that are killing you. Take your kids out of school and let them do and learn whatever they want to in a safe environment. You don't need anyone's permission.

If it's not enjoyable or productive, quit or don't go to college in the first place. Step up and out into the world in which you want to live. Work with interesting people, read interesting books, do interesting things. There's no need to pay for someone else's stamp on someone else's set of activities just because everyone else does.

You don't need a degree to do what you want. You may choose to get one. You may decide it's worth the trade-offs. You may enjoy it. Do it if you do, but don't ever do it "because you have to." You don't have to. Create a way to do what you want without it. It's harder, but freedom is always harder than the comfort of captivity.

Get off the conveyor belt

The reason many people fear opting out is because of a paradigm of linear, externally-defined progress that I call the conveyor belt mentality. This mentality is holding you back and must be demolished. It goes something like this:

You are plopped onto a production line at whatever stage you're supposed to be based on arbitrary things like your age, class, and gender. Then you let the belt do the work. By essentially doing nothing but what you're told, you get handed certificates at each next stage. 18? Unless you did something truly outrageous, here's your diploma. 22? Here's your degree. Degree? Here's your job (or so you're led to believe).

Most people believe this and live it. It's revealed in the kinds of questions we ask strangers. "What grade are you in?" "What's your major?" "What kind of job do you have?" If your answer is not the appropriate one for your age and assumed station in life, people worry. "I dropped out of school to do X" is cause for concern to almost everybody, no matter what X is. "I'm a sophomore at university Y" is cause for comfort to almost everybody, no matter what you're actually doing with your time at Y. So long as you're at your station, no one much cares if you're productive, happy, successful, fulfilled, or free.

Parents obsessively check their child against a list of averages on everything from height to reading ability and stress if junior is not "on track." No one really ever asks who built the track, where it's going, or whether junior has any interest in arriving there.

The conveyor belt sucks. It's not taking you where you want to go. Aggregates are not individuals, and your goals and abilities are not definable by summing the abilities and behaviors of everyone your age and dividing by the population size. Time to get off.

It's scary at first, because your mind is trained to think that progress is defined by moving on the conveyor belt in the only direction it goes. Maybe really special or hard working people go faster, like the people who run up an escalator instead of letting the machine do all the work, but everyone is channelled in the same narrow corral moving in the same direction. That's not progress.

Progress, for you, is moving towards your own goals and desires and becoming more fulfilled as you grow and overcome challenges. There are as many directions as there are people. Once you jump off the conveyor belt, the hardest part is actually discovering what makes you come alive, then being honest and unashamed of what you discover. It's worth it. You can never start too soon.

The thing is, the mold-breakers who jump the belt don't struggle any more or less than those who stay on. They have a hard time too. But it's a different kind of pain. It's the pain of working to achieve a goal they're passionate about that has huge rewards when won, not the pain of subjugation to a monotony that brings nothing in return.

Work vs. play

Once you jump the belt, a number of other paradigms are shattered, like the dichotomy between work and play.

The best play is hard work, and the most productive work is hard play. This is pretty intuitive for small children absent the school system. Their play is sometimes torturous to watch. They struggle and struggle to reach a high object or beat a video game, often showing great emotional and physical angst. No one is making them. They are playing.

The best workers in any field are doing something akin to child's play. They are delighted, the outside world almost non-existent, as they push themselves to produce and create and solve problems. This is true in even the most inglorious work. I recall a coworker at a grocery store when I was a teen who would challenge me in various grocery bagging games. We would sweat and work and struggle to achieve speed and accuracy while keeping the customer happy. The hours flew by when we worked together, and the managers loved us. It was hard but so much more fun than the days I worked

with those content to do the minimum accept-
able, or when I didn't push myself.

Work and play are both temporary games we
enter into by choice, with rules and norms and
goals that may or may not have any meaning
outside of the game. Both involve repetition of
certain activities and the acquisition of skill in
the process, as well as exploration, innovation,
collaboration, and creative problem solving.

Even if your work is "just to make a buck" so
you can spend time and money doing other
non-paid activities, it can still be play. I didn't
bag groceries for the good of humanity or just
because it was fun. I did it do earn money so I
could travel and do other things, but I still ben-
efitted from breaking down the work/play dichotomy.

Work and education are also inseparable. Because of the schooling paradigm, we often separate education from work and treat them as
distinct activities to go with distinct stations on
the conveyor belt. Work and and education are
both a mix of playful exploration and disci-
plined mastery, but all by choice and either for
pleasure or for another end that you've chosen.
Choice is the key word.

If we want to meaningfully define work as something separate from education or play, I think we could say that work involves producing something not just for your own consumption. It's the act of producing something that creates value for others so that you may exchange it to get something else you want but cannot produce yourself. It is highly collaborative.

I meet a lot of people who would love to produce certain things or work with certain people but who assume they lack the credentials. The secret is that, in the end, the only credential that matters is the value you create.

Rational choice theory instead of good vs. evil

Once you've identified problems with the schooling worldview, the conveyor belt mindset, and the permission based approach to production, it's easy to feel like there is a giant conspiracy at work to keep you down. Be careful not to take this idea too seriously. Whether or not anyone is conspiring to dupe you into a cog-like existence, believing that nefarious forces are behind it is disempowering. To effectively navigate the world and achieve your own ends, you need to move beyond simplistic tales of good and evil. People and institutions needn't be bad in order to do things detrimental to you, and they needn't be good to prove helpful.

The most effective tool for understanding and predicting human behavior is rational choice theory. It's what economists use to explain both individual behavior and the broader order that results. Rational choice theory is nothing more than the assumption that every person is a self-interested rational actor. They act only when they believe doing so will help them achieve their ends better than inaction or any alternative action. It makes no judgement of the rightness or wrongness of their interests.

It sounds simple, but once you look at the world this way, it forces you to dig deeper and solve mysteries. It won't let you off the hook with unhelpful explanations like, "There's no way to deal with that person. They're just crazy!" Whether or not you agree with their preferences, there is an internal logic to their choices, and if you want to avoid problems, it's best to understand it.

You may object that, though rational choice theory can help you understand people who are acting to get what they want and not just to torment you for torment's sake, aren't there people who are genuinely evil and truly revel in your misery? How can rational choice account for this? Isn't it impossible to understand what they're aiming at and negotiate to avoid pain?

I had a friend who felt totally helpless when dealing with a person she worked with who was always late. She was convinced that this person could not be reasoned with or avoided. She thought the coworker irrationally wanted to sabotage her progress and was 30 minutes late on purpose to ensure it happened.

If we grant that the person is irrational, pure evil, hell bent on her discomfort, this theory has provided no explanatory power for the particular actions taken. Why didn't the person just slash her tires if inconveniencing her was the goal? Why did they show up 30 minutes late, instead of 60, or not at all? What accounts for the particular choices made? Clearly, some kind of calculation was involved. Even if being a jerk was the goal, the person must have reasoned that showing up 30 minutes late was the least costly way to exact the most jerkiness. In other words, they looked at costs and benefits and made a rational choice given their preferences.

Once you strip away the emotion and realize that, evil or not, people still make rational choices about what means to employ in seeking their ends, anger and helplessness tends to melt away. If the person was rational enough to choose whether to be late and by how much, does it seem probable they did it just to tick you off? Not in most cases. Far more likely, they had a phone call, forgot to get gas ahead of time, failed to account for traffic, or any number of other things, and they determined sacrificing 30 minutes was the least bad solution.

But even if they wanted to cause trouble, knowing they have a cost/benefit calculation just like you do can help you see possible workarounds. How might you change their incentives to improve the chances of punctuality? The onus is on you to accept their preferences, whether you like them or not, and learn to get what you want anyway.

It's much easier emotionally to just call them evil and irrational and propagate the myth of your own helplessness. It might feel good in the moment, but it's a terrible way to reach your goals, and it fails to explain the real world. In fact, the vindictiveness that can result is likely to make them truly angry with you, whether they were at first or not. It might make them want to exact revenge, just perpetuating the conflict.

Treat the conflict as a game. Worry less about the morality of others or their motives and put more focus on what caused them to choose what they did and how you might alter what they view as in their best interest. You'll enjoy life more, and you might find people around you aren't as bad as you think.

Experiencing bad outcomes created by people or systems doesn't need to make you feel bitter or helpless. Treat them as rational responses to the perverse incentives present and you'll begin to find your way over, around, or through them.

It's all about value

Lest you think the point of this section is that, if you get your mindset right, you'll gain career success and material wealth, let me clear that up right now. No mindset will automatically produce wealth, career flexibility, or fulfill-ment. The only thing that matters is creating value.

A lot of self-help and get-rich books talk about a paradigm of plenty or various visualization techniques to gain wealth or career freedom. This is all fine and good and probably useful once you have some success already, but at the end of the day you can't obtain any wealth or success in the market unless you create value.

I don't mean "value" in any objective sense. Economic value is subjective. If you want people to give you their money, time, resources, and even respect, there is but one way to get it (outside of the violent approach thieves and governments prefer), and that is through ex-change. No one will voluntarily enter an ex-change unless he believes that he is gaining more value than they are giving up.

The way to succeed, then, is to constantly ask what you can do that other people value. Who values it? How much? How can you let them know? What else might you do that's valued even more, or by a greater number of people? How might you replicate the things you can do that are valuable to others and distribute them more broadly? Can you systematize how you or others create value and make it more efficient?

Creating value can take any form. It may be making someone laugh, or solving a mundane problem, or saving a life, or easing an emotional burden. Whatever way you do it, you can't let yourself forget that value creation, not positive thinking or living in the right city, is ultimately the only way to gain value for yourself.

Don't wait for permission to create value

"I'm looking for a job right now. I really like what you're doing, so let me know if there's any opportunities or open positions to help you grow it. I'd like to find something in the next month where I can use my skills and experience. Not sure if you're hiring, but thought I'd check!"

I've gotten plenty of emails like this, and I'm not alone. The thing is, I don't believe them. If you really want to work with someone, why wait until you have permission via an official job title? Why not do anything you can to create value now?

Contrast the email above with this:

"I love what you're doing and I want to help in any way that I can. I'll work for free. I can provide content for your social media pages, write blog posts, copy-edit newsletters, do market research, and take care of anything else you need. Here's a quick image I created for you to use and examples of some of my other work. Give me a project to start working on!"

I've only ever gotten two emails like this. Both of them got a quick response after I saw proof that they weren't crazy and could do good work. Both of them got hired not long after.

This isn't a formula to landing a job but an example of two different mindsets. The first email asks for a paycheck. It asks for permission to be added to the payroll and given official duties. The second email begs to create value and in fact shares value already created. You don't need an official job offer, title, or paycheck to begin creating value in areas that make you come alive or to work with people you want to be around. Just do it.

It reminds me of the people who say they really want to be writers. You can't want to be a writer. A writer is someone who writes. You either write or you don't. To want to write but not do it is to not really want it. Create value. Make yourself indispensable. If you are, you will get paid, and probably better than you could elsewhere.

When people are in "job search" mode and tweaking resumes, waiting for interview calls, surfing the job boards, and so on, they tend to slip into a permission-based mindset. "If only someone else gives me permission, I can do work I enjoy and earn money." I sometimes suggest that they create some value for free, and the reaction is usually, "but why would I do that?" The real question is "why wouldn't you?" The burden of proof is on the person waiting around, with low opportunity cost, to prove why they shouldn't just start working, officially or not.

"I need X to be a Y"

No, you don't.

For the longest time, I had entrepreneurial urges. I had a lot of different startup ideas, but I didn't have a lot of business connections or capital, so I couldn't be an entrepreneur. At some point (sadly later than I wish), I realized that entrepreneurship is not an ontological status but an activity. You're either building a business and creating a vision or you're not. There is no prerequisite to entrepreneurial action.

Entrepreneurs begin moving the project forward and do something every day to push it ahead and add value. All the trappings — the business plan, the logo, the mission statement, the money, the customers, the employees, the org chart, the management techniques — come along the way. You don't need to get on bended knee and be knighted "Sir Entrepreneur" before you can build something.

I use entrepreneur as my example because I think it is the ultimate form of worker all of us want to be. In this sense, I mean it as a kind of activity, not narrowly as someone who founded or owns a business. An entrepreneur is someone who is not just repeating known actions and implementing known solutions, but who is creatively problem solving. You can act entrepreneurially in any job. Be careful — it's addictive. The more you see everything around you as negotiable and improvable, you'll want a wider and wider scope for freedom in your work. Good. Create it.

"Entrepreneur" is the word that in many ways sums up the philosophy of this book. It's someone who sometimes plays the game, sometimes opts out, and sometimes, when it's worth it, changes the game. You don't need anything but to do it.

How to find what you love

You want to be truly alive. You want your work, education, and life to be fulfilling. How to discover what makes you come alive? It's a process, but it's actually much easier than you think. Here's the only rule you need to follow:

Don't do things you don't like doing.

That's it. You don't need to find out what you do like, because it's a moving target and because many things you'll end up loving haven't been invented yet. As long as you try a lot of things and stay away from those you don't enjoy, you're moving in the right direction.

Surprisingly, this is really hard to put into practice. Maybe it's the Puritan ideal that suffering through drudgery purges the soul, or maybe it's the guilt, shame, fear, and obligation we allow ourselves to take on from others in the name of altruism. Whatever the cause, we are surrounded with inner and outer voices that subtly nudge our decisions and activities into a lot of things that we really don't enjoy at all. If you step back and ask, "Do I actually want to be doing this?" you might be surprised how many things would get a "no."

Of course this is different than not doing anything hard or even painful. I ran a marathon once. The training sucked. Many times while running, I felt I would rather be sitting on the couch with a beer. But I didn't actually want that. I wanted it in a vacuum, but the real world has trade-offs. In the world of trade-offs, though I wanted to drink beer and sit on the couch, I wanted to be able to finish a marathon more. Thus, I endured pain and hardship because I wanted what it would bring me more than I wanted the alternatives.

In order to not do things you don't like, you need ruthless self-knowledge and self-honesty. Do I really not want to do this thing, or do I only not want to do it compared with some other imagined option that is imagined? It forces you to not feel embarrassed about what you discover.

Once I internalized this lesson, I made it one of my daily, weekly, and long-term goals to continually reduce the numbers of things I do that I do not enjoy. Perhaps surprisingly, the more I focused on and succeeded at this, the more hard work I ended up doing. You might imagine pursuing this goal would result in me sitting around a lot (with beer and football), but it turns out that when you're doing things you like, you actually want to work, and you work well. I became more and more productive.

Consider the biggest stressors and pain points in your life. Stop doing them as soon as possible.

Go get it

Your learning, growing, producing, and exchanging are playful, challenging processes. You own them. The traditional accoutrements are tools to be used if and when they get you what you want. Don't just default to them. Take charge and create the kind of life you want.

Keeping It Real: Exercises in Inner-Freedom
T.K. Coleman

"The most common way people give up their power is by thinking they don't have any." - Alice Walker

I believe that instead of being victims of circumstance, we can choose to become champions of creativity. The fact that our problems are real should never be mistaken for evidence that our power is fake. Mental and emotional freedom has nothing to do with denying reality. It has everything to do with remembering that reality is a vast realm that also encompasses our potential to cope with difficulties and create new possibilities. In our effort to be honest about our problems, it is not necessary that we cease to be mindful of our potential.

One of the most common concerns people have about philosophies that tell us of our power to live freely is the fear that they must choose to be delusional in order to be optimistic. To be fair, much of this concern is rooted in the fact that some people do seem to approach optimism in this sort of way. We are all too familiar with self-help gurus, motivational speakers, television personalities, and pollyanna friends who tell us to "be positive" or to "turn our frowns upside down." The thinking person has every right to be leery of any message that explicitly says or implies that we should never admit to feeling bad or that we should never acknowledge our problems.

If by "positive thinking" one means "forcing yourself to smile no matter how you feel," or "forcing yourself to speak triumphantly regardless of what you truly think," or "using the power of affirmations to magically make unwanted circumstances disappear," then we should, by all means, abandon "positive thinking."

As an alternative to "positive thinking," I invite you to consider the value of philosophical thinking.

According to Marilyn Adams, philosophical thinking is the process of "thinking really hard about the most important questions and trying to bring analytic clarity both to the questions and the answers." Philosophy isn't a comprehensive system that tells us what to believe, but it's a way of thinking that challenges us to entertain alternative ways of seeing things. Philosophy is an invitation to take our common sense perceptions of reality and ask ourselves questions like "Why do I believe this?" and "What are some other plausible ways I can look at this?"

My approach to mental and emotional freedom, which I refer to as Tough-Minded Optimism, is based on the application of philosophical thinking to the following three categories.

1) Truth
2) Positivity
3) Happiness

While it won't be possible to say everything (or even most things) that can be said about these three categories, my goal is to challenge some conventional attitudes about these themes in an effort to show that by expanding our ideas on truth, positivity, and happiness, we can lay the beginnings of a solid foundation for a freer life.

Truth

Keeping It Real

The comedian Dave Chappelle once did a segment on his hourly sketch show titled "When keeping it real goes wrong."

The segment involved someone who was the victim of some minor slight directed at him by an insensitive party. At the precise moment of the offense, the victim would be faced with a dilemma: do they choose to let things slide and "keep it cool" or do they "keep it real" by retaliating? Of course, with this being a comedy sketch, the victim would always choose to keep it real.

Unfortunately, there was usually some factor at play that the victim could not have anticipated. Perhaps the person they lashed back at was a third degree black belt in martial arts who was out looking for a good fight. Whatever the particulars, it suffices to say that "keeping it real" always ended in a humiliating manner for the slighted person.

This sketch provides a humorous yet poignant illustration of how unnecessarily troublesome life can get when one's particular understanding of what it means to "keep it real" is left unchecked by rational scrutiny. The cause of trouble in each example in the skit was someone's belief that engaging in a fruitless act of rage or revenge was tantamount to "being truthful."

This supposition is not far from popular conceptions of what it means to be a truthful person. Because speaking in the language of niceties and positive-sounding cliches is such an easy way to avoid conflict, the willingness to say something negative or contrarian is frequently and understandably associated with truth. When we say things like, "I have a friend who tells it like it is," we usually mean "I have a friend who isn't afraid to say things that are difficult to hear." While there's nothing inherently wrong with this fact, it's important to ask ourselves, "Is there a necessary relationship between Truth and Negativity?" While we might be more inclined to believe people who freely say negative things (after all, since there's no obvious reward for telling bad news, why would someone say it unless it were true?), our inclinations aren't always a reliable indicator of truth. Philosophically speaking, truth exists independently of our motives for believing in it.

In other words, true statements don't magically become false just because we want them to be true. And false statements don't magically become true just because we feel confident and courageous enough to say them.

A casual watching of any horror movie will reveal that there are lots of scary ideas that are untrue. If there really were monsters living underneath my bed, it would most certainly benefit me to "keep it real" about that fact. However, it is simply not the case that monsters are living under my bed. "Keeping it real" in this instance would involve my honest acknowledgment of the fact that my bedroom is a safe place to sleep. This truth is not compromised by the fact that I take great comfort from knowing it. Nor is this truth cheapened by the fact that, deep down inside, this is what I strongly prefer to believe. If I were to deny the unreality of "mattress monsters" just because I wanted to prove myself to be a daring soul who follows the truth wherever it leads, I would actually be committing a grave act of intellectual dishonesty. This observation underscores a key principle to achieving inner-freedom:

The truth is the truth, even when it's not negative.

In virtually any discussion on taking charge of one's life and living freely, someone is almost guaranteed to utter some variation of the following:

"Optimism is good, but it's also important to be honest and not delude ourselves about the real stuff that's going on in the world."

Usually, when these sorts of statements are made, the word "honest" means "negative" and the term "real stuff" means "bad stuff."

I get it. It's a wise sentiment. It makes a great deal of sense and it needs to be said.

But...

Here's something else that needs to be said if we're going to have an honest discussion about being honest:

Being realistic encompasses the negative, but it by no means excludes the positive.

If you focus on the world's deficiencies and stop there, then you'll probably feel horrible and paralyzed. But why stop there? It's intellectually dishonest to focus on what's wrong with the world without acknowledging our rich history of overcoming incredible odds.

At any given moment, the universe is infinitely larger than than the particular point of view we hold. There are always insights you haven't heard before. There are always techniques you haven't been exposed to yet. There are always practices you haven't learned yet. There are always skills you haven't developed yet. There are always stories that you haven't read yet about people who have gone through related struggles. There are always questions you haven't considered yet.

"Keeping it real" isn't just a matter of facing up to harsh facts. It also includes opening up to the plethora of possibilities that offer us ways of impacting the world in spite of adversity. The path to freedom, then, is not self-delusional optimism but rather a commitment to following the truth so relentlessly that you refuse to arbitrarily exalt your perception of negativity over the practical ideas and positive insights that can help you move forward.

Mental and emotional freedom is not the denial of truth — it's the recognition that truth isn't something we need to run from or be afraid of. When you realize that Truth is an infinitely large category of which your problems and frustrations are only a subset, you can face the truth with confidence, composure, and even a sense of childlike curiosity.

When Keeping it Real Goes Wrong (The Fallacy of Misdirected Attention)

If focusing on a particular truth makes you feel like crap, that's not an excuse for you to ignore it. After all, regardless of how it makes you feel, if it's something that you need to hear, then it's important to face reality. If the truth is that you have been diagnosed with an illness, it would behoove you to inform yourself about that illness and its implications for your life as much as possible.

Unfortunately, this observation tends to get conflated with the following idea:

"If something is true, regardless of how bad it makes you feel, you are morally and rationally obligated to pay attention to it regardless of context. The corollary of this idea is that you are uninformed or delusional if you are not privy to current events merely because such things are disturbing or uninteresting to you."

This is what I refer to as the "but it's true fallacy."

"But it's true," in this sense, is usually short for "Since it's true, it must be important or beneficial to talk about," or "Because it's true, it would be wrong for you to ignore it."

That statement is the pessimist's ultimate trump card. It allows them to say anything, no matter how negative without the pressure of having to justify themselves.

Try asking a pessimist to stop talking about the negative aspect of things, and they will not only play the "but it's true" card, but they'll also make you feel like a delusional dopehead who needs to get your head out of the sand.

Such a statement is supposed to leave the rest of us speechless. After all, what else can you do once someone says "but it's true," other than shrug your shoulders and say "you're right"?

But how might we apply philosophical thinking to this issue? One question we can ask is, "Are all truthful propositions equally worthy of our attention irrespective of context?"

Imagine the following scenario:

I'm sitting in a business meeting with a potential investor discussing my company's shareholder agreement.

The investor-prospect asks, "T.K., can you explain the meaning of the second sentence in the first paragraph on page two?"

I randomly respond by saying, "I had pancakes for breakfast this morning!"

The prospect gives me a weird look and then replies, "...and what does that have to do with my question about the shareholder agreement?"

"Well, I don't know," I say defensively. "But it's true! I really did have pancakes for breakfast this morning!"

If the above scenario sounds a little off, that's because it should.

It sounds off because of a basic distinction we all recognize between "truthfulness" and "relevance."

"Truthfulness" is the quality of someone who accurately reports facts.

"Relevance" is the attribute of something that is usable or related to the matter at hand.

Being truthful is not the same as being relevant.

What I have to say may be factual, but that doesn't mean my facts are going to be useful, helpful, or connected to the things that matter to the audience I'm addressing.

In my above scenario, the statement "I had pancakes for breakfast this morning" was true, but in relation to my potential investor's concerns it was irrelevant.

It may have been relevant to me. After all, I get to decide what's important to me.

The investor, on the other hand, is under no obligation to indulge ideas that are irrelevant to him, nor does he need to feel guilty for refusing to do so.

If you randomly call a friend and say, "I'm jumping rope while wearing a pair of blue gym shoes," they will probably ask something along the lines of "why are you telling me this?" If your response is, "I'm just telling you the facts. Stop being so delusional," it is quite likely that your friend will be more than a bit confused. "But it's true" has never been a satisfactory answer to the question "what is your point?"

Here are two vital observations about truth:

1) The size of Truth is inexhaustible: In any given moment, there are literally millions of facts to which we can give our attention. There is literally no known end to the amount of factual statements that we can discuss at any given moment. No matter what you choose to think about or talk about, your perspective will always leave millions of facts, good and bad, out of the discussion. Right now you are unconsciously overlooking or deliberately ignoring tons of facts about the world, and there is simply no way to avoid this predicament. Hence it is impossible to ever have a comprehensive awareness of truth. We can be honest in our dealings with truth but never exhaustive.

2) The relevance of any particular truth-claim is contextual. While there may be an aesthetic sense in which truth is inherently good, beautiful, or valuable, from a practical point of view, facts depend quite heavily on context for their meaning.

The implication of these two truths about truth is that you can't focus on everything and that, of all the things you're capable of focusing on, it is not the case that everything is relevant to your priorities, abilities, and responsibilities.

This brings me to my second insight regarding how a bit of philosophical reflection about truth can help you understand things in a way that leads to a freer life.

You will never be mentally and emotionally free as long as you allow others to convince you that they are free to dump their garbage on you whenever they want without regard to context, timing, setting, purpose, etc., merely because they are reporting statements that happen to be factually correct. Liberty is a lifestyle that cannot happen until you define for yourself what it means to "be informed."

There are many sources of information that are eager to inform you of the latest horror story that took place somewhere in the universe. And even though these horror stories may frighten you, depress you, or stress you out, these "news outlets" feel quite proud of themselves for telling you anyway because, after all, it's true!

Contrary to the "but it's true fallacy," however, you're being delusional only if you ignore something that you actually need to pay attention to.

If you're choosing to ignore a message of doom and gloom because it doesn't benefit you or anyone else for you to be aware of it and because your time, energy, and focus are better spent on constructive things, then you're not being delusional. You're being deliberate. You're being conscious of how you use your time. You're being healthy. You're being responsible and intelligent.

Some truths, whether they feel good to listen to or not, are things you need to know. However, there are also some truths, including so-called negative ones, that you don't need to know. Ultimately, you have to be the one who decides what kind of information diet best serves you.

This is not about other people's right to report whatever facts they wish to report. It's about your right to decide what you should focus on.

I believe in freedom of speech. I do not believe in the mindless consumption of every piece of factual data that's put in front of our faces.

Cultivating inner-freedom means being deliberate about the stories you consume and the ideas in which you indulge.

Whether they are negative or positive isn't what's important. What's important is that you are in charge of the process of putting your attention on the things you need to focus on.

Positivity

In a nutshell, my message to the world is this: quit trying so darn hard to be positive.

Inner-freedom is neither about making positive assumptions nor about forcing yourself to feel good. Inner-freedom is simply the art of remaining open to possibility. What happens when we are no longer occupying the mind with our judgments, labels, and dogmatic opinions? When we are not trying to artificially make ourselves believe that life is great and when we are not busy assuming that it's the end of the world, we are left with nothing but possibility. That state of being open to possibility without judgment is the source of creative power, personal growth, and inner-freedom.

Positive assumptions are needed only when you have negative assumptions that you're trying to overcome. But when you drop your assumptions altogether, your soul stands naked in the open fields of possibility. And what you choose to create from that space is up to you.

"I don't believe in therapy. I don't believe in positive thinking. I don't believe that church communities, 12-step programs, or self-help groups will benefit me. I don't believe in western medicine. I don't believe in alternative medicine and holistic health. I don't believe in hard work. I don't believe in entrepreneurship. I don't believe in meditation.I don't believe in physical fitness programs. I don't believe in behavioral psychology, attachment theory, gestalt therapy, or neuro-linguistic programming. I don't believe in the seven highly effective habits, the Silva Method, or EST. I don't believe in gurus. I don't believe in that author, or that expert, or that book, or that person's testimonial. I do not believe!"

I hear statements like this all the time from real people who are hungry for practical solutions to their problems. When confronted with practical suggestions for how they can change their lives, they immediately go into a monologue about what they don't believe. For many of these people, a lack of belief in something is, all by itself, enough reason to dismiss new proposals without discussion. When people declare their list of non-beliefs to me, my response is usually, "well, luckily, inner-freedom is not a religion and there are no belief requirements you need to meet in order to qualify." The willingness to explore the unfamiliar is far more pivotal than the ability to make oneself believe in the objective, absolute truth of a particular theory, philosophy, or therapeutic technique.

Instead of trying to make yourself believe in something bigger and better, try taking more chances on activities and practices that offer you the opportunity to make new discoveries. This is how creativity differs from positive thinking. Positive thinking is the attitude of one who believes in the probability of a positive outcome. Creativity is the determination to act towards a desired goal, however unconventional the means, whether the results are guaranteed or not.

Maybe things will get better, maybe they won't. Maybe your ideas will work, maybe they won't. Maybe you'll have a good time, maybe you won't. There's no need to torture yourself over what to believe. Create and see. Live and learn. Work and watch. Experiment and evaluate.

If you truly want to learn and grow, you don't need unwavering faith in positivity as much you need a sense of wonder, a spirit of adventure, and a mild dissatisfaction with the status quo. Faith is overrated. The willingness to try something new is everything.

Inner-freedom isn't about fitting any one person's definition of what it means to be positive. It's about finding whatever approach works for you in the quest to create the kind of life you truly love. It's far more important that you develop your own process for creating desired results than to strive to outdo the guy who walks around with a smile on his face seven days a week. If having a serious face helps you to focus more, then the smiles can wait for a later time. If you've found a way to successfully channel the feeling of anger along creative lines, may the force be with you. Forget about the positivity stereotypes. Trying to conform to them is a distraction. The value of your life isn't determined by how positive others think you are but by what works and feels right for you.

Happiness

"I love myself when I am laughing. . . and then again when I am looking mean and impressive." -Zora Neale Hurston

Inner-freedom is less about feeling good and more about learning to develop a healthy and harmonious relationship with the variety of emotional states you're likely to occupy over the course of a lifetime.

I refer to this process as the art of emotional versatility. Emotional versatility is the art of making peace with the entire emotional spectrum by honing your capacity to channel various feelings along creative and constructive lines. It is not about controlling or condemning your feelings. It's about conducting your feelings in a self-edifying way. In contrast to philosophies that encourage us to passively accept whatever we feel as "good," emotional versatility says "make friends with your feelings by actively integrating all of your psychological experiences into the larger context of your life as creative process."

Instead of viewing yourself as a static repository waiting for the universe to deposit "positive" emotions into your soul, you can approach life from the orientation of a dynamic creator who is constantly involved in an ongoing process of building, innovating, and altering his or her world.

In the former view, your feelings are your life. In the latter view, the creative process is your life, and your feelings, whether "good" or "bad," are a form of fuel than can be used to amplify, accelerate, or augment the creative process. This is precisely what some musicians claim to do when they use a heartbreaking experience as material for a song.

Emotional versatility extends this concept to cover life as a whole. Working with the metaphor of "life as art," emotional versatility presupposes a concept of personal freedom that says "as a personal agent, you are a creative force. You are free to the extent that you are able to control your focus, channel your feelings, and conduct your actions in a manner that is conducive to creating the results that matter most to you."

Rumi wrote:

"Dance, when you're broken open. Dance, if you've torn the bandage off. Dance in the middle of the fighting. Dance in your blood. Dance when you're perfectly free."

Happiness is like a genre of music that nearly everyone knows how to dance to. Happiness has a very simple tempo, catchy phrasing, and memorable lyrics. It's the song at the wedding that makes everyone excited to run to the dance floor.

Most of our so-called positive emotions would fall into this category. In the same way that no one runs around searching frantically for a dance instructor when a song only demands "lift your hands and shout," we rarely find people looking for a therapist when they feel happy.

What happens, however, when the D.J. stops playing the easy party music and chooses to switch things over to some other more complex or unfamiliar form of music? Some people just keep on dancing as if nothing has changed. Some people stand around looking awkwardly. Some complain about the D.J. Some leave the dance floor until an easier tune comes back on.

This is analogous to what happens when we begin to feel "negative" emotions: we gradually shift from a state of playfully or calmly expressing our "positive" feelings to complaining, giving up, pretending like nothing has changed, or doing the hard work of figuring out how to cope. When the music demands something that the dancer is untrained to do, the dancer will either quit or commit himself to navigating the challenge. This latter choice is what the art of emotional versatility encourages us to do with our "negative" feelings.

We must recognize that our frustrations are largely due to the fact that we have not learned how to "dance" to a large part of the emotional spectrum. Being emotionally versatile is like being a good dancer. Just as dancers must challenge themselves to master new moves with their bodies, we must challenge ourselves to learn new forms of psychological choreography.

We all must strive to find our own ways, however quirky and unsexy those efforts may be, of moving to the unorthodox rhythms of anger, sadness, jealousy, or any other style of emotion that tends to trip us up or throw us off.

The problem with feelings is neither that our moods fluctuate nor that our emotions seem to fail us. The greater dilemma is that most have only learned how to dance to one type of feeling.

From the vantage point of the creative orientation, all feelings are a form of psychological energy capable of being harnessed for productive purposes. As in art-making, the goal of emotional versatility isn't to gain victory over our so-called negative feelings but to enlist them as our allies in a battle that involves much more than merely feeling good. Our feelings are not there to be cast out or conquered. They're there to be engaged and expressed with imagination and intelligence.

Inner-freedom is the resolve to be defined by our capacity to create rather than by the particular mood we happen to be in at a given moment. When we primarily identify ourselves as "feelers," our capacity to create or even "get through the day" becomes dependent on what we feel. When we feel powerful and brilliant, we express those feelings through creative endeavor. When we feel like losers, we behave accordingly. When we primarily identify as "creators," we give context to our feelings. Our feelings are no longer the main event and our intentions take center stage. And even though our feelings may sometimes seem "negative," they never betray us because we always have the opportunity to integrate them into our creative process.

C.S. Lewis once wrote, "the man who tries to measure how quickly he's falling asleep is likely to remain awake all night." Such is the fate of those who obsess over their emotional state. If you're spending most of your time and energy measuring how you feel, you'll likely remain stuck in your current condition. As William Coyne observed, "After you plant a seed in the ground, you don't don't dig it up every week to see how it is doing." Just as an entrepreneur is likely to fail if all he thinks about is money, you are likely to remain unfree if all you think about is your feelings. Just as the entrepreneur makes profits by shifting his thinking from "how do I get more money?" to "how can I create wealth for others?" we find inner-freedom by shifting our predominant focus from "what am I feeling?" to "what am I creating?"

If you want to create a free life without asking for permission, you have to decide that you're going to be the kind of person who thinks, speaks, and acts creatively regardless of mood. When you make this fundamental choice, your feelings will stop controlling you. They'll start collaborating with you.

Conclusion

The purpose of this collection was not to present a cohesive theory of political freedom but a framework for thinking about your own personal emancipation. Political freedom is the most obvious — and oftentimes the most pressing — form of freedom, but freedom is ultimately a deeply personal project.

The fruits of political freedom wither when we throw off the chains of tyrants only to hook ourselves up to less-obvious systems of unfreedom — whether they be electoral politics, school and career, or even our own worldviews.

There's no reason to limit yourself to your political dogma, your major, or your feelings at any given moment. The world you act within is in a constant state of invention and reinvention. As a subject within it, so are you.

Stop waiting for permission to invent your world and your life. Freedom starts with your

own emancipation — something only you can
seize.

About the Authors

TK Coleman

TK Coleman is the Education Director for Praxis. Through his work as an entrepreneur and educator, he strives to promote the idea that creativity and critical thinking are the keys to living freely and building a better world. TK's life mission is to persuade as many people as possible that they have the permission and power to be the predominant creative force in their lives.

Isaac Morehouse

Isaac Morehouse is an entrepreneur, thinker, and communicator dedicated to the relentless pursuit of freedom. He is the founder and CEO of Praxis, an intensive ten-month program combining real-world business experience with the best of online education for those who want more than college.

Christopher Nelson

Christopher Nelson is a writer, researcher, and educator. Originally from California, Christopher spent many years at the Institute for Humane Studies at George Mason University before working at the University of Arizona and finally moving to the midwest. He has a Bachelor's degree from UCLA and a Master's degree from the Catholic University of America, in Washington, DC. The ideas of liberty have offered Christopher the greatest adventure and most rewarding education of all.

Zachary Slayback

Zachary Slayback is an Ivy League dropout and the Business Development Director for Praxis. He is a regular commentator on issues concerning education, entrepreneurship, and social change. His writings have appeared in *The Christian Science Monitor, The Huffington Post, The Daily Caller, Business Insider,* and other outlets. He has appeared as a guest on *HuffPost Live* and *The Glenn Beck Program.*

Made in the USA
Las Vegas, NV
23 February 2023